Relationships

Ninety-Two Tried and True Ways to Damage or Fatally Destroy Your Relationship

Charmaine Richards

Edited by: Pothier, June, Charmaine, Beverley, Marjorie, Donna and Kerry-Kay

authorHOUSE®

AuthorHouse™
1663 Liberty Drive
Bloomington, IN 47403
www.authorhouse.com
Phone: 1-800-839-8640

First published by AuthorHouse 5/10/2011

ISBN: 978-1-4520-2324-3 (sc)
ISBN: 978-1-4520-2325-0 (e)

Library of Congress Control Number: 2010907217

Printed in the United States of America
Bloomington, Indiana

This book is printed on acid-free paper.

Acknowledgement

Heartfelt love and everlasting thanks first and foremost to my mother and late father, (maa and papa) for their never ending love, care, acceptance and support; my wonderful sister, Pothier (Dinghy Dawny), for her relentless typing and scouting out publishers. Once even staying up all night typing and cooking.

Thanks to my nephew, Leighton (Kev), *'Mr. Cool'* for his expert computer skills.

To my awesome siblings, Winston, Beverley, Pothier, Joan, Marjorie, Daniel and David for their constant love and support.

To my nieces, Nichelle, and Roshelle and my nephew Adrian for their shots of confidence. *"Auntie Charm, your book is cool. I love it! My friends would love to read it."*

To Donna, Keisha, Shirley (Dimple) and Trevor for their constant support and encouragement.

To other family members for their encouragement and support.

To all my aunts, uncles and cousins for believing in me.

To my special friend W.T. *(Peta)* for everything.

To my great friends who have been supportive throughout the years.

To my wonderful god-daughters Kailey and Ljhauren.

Thanks to my god-son Krhystof as well as, Knyckolas and Stacey for their typing.

Thanks

to all my friends especially my circle of best friends for
their continuous love, support and encouragement.

Peta	Charmaine
Ann-Marie	Angella
Olive	Winston
Leroy	Jacqueline
Dionne	Hazel
Navia	Mama Betty
Diana	Brian
Heather	Naida
Stacey	Audrey
Joy	Norma
Cecile	Debra
Mark	Robert
Oscar	Navlette
Tyrone	Ann
Aunt Icy	Nathan
Tiffany	

<u>My Mentors</u>

My Parents- Mr. amd Mrs. L. Richards
Bishop Neville B. Currie
Barbara
Dr. Bhatia
Winston, Missionary Bradford and Kristan

Dedicated to: my nieces and nephews

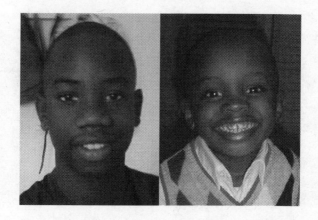

Introduction

Studies show that health and work can contribute to happiness but social relations and connections are the key to happiness. Self help is the major pathway to how most of us grow. I think there is nothing more wonderful and fulfilling than a respectful caring relationship. But of course, mistakes and blunders are inevitable.

Dealing with life's problems can be hard work so if you can't bare the thought of messing up your tidy soul you won't make it as a human being.

As you read this book, remember, everyone makes mistakes. Identify your weaknesses and work on your strengths in order to develop your character.

Relationships are complicated, with their jealousies, insecurities and sensitivities, to name a few.

With love, commitment and care nothing is impossible.

Love is an action word so give up your right to get even with whomever for whatever and get busy loving in one or many ways.

Relationships

92 Tried and True Ways
to Damage or Fatally
Destroy Your Relationship

1. Stay emotionally immature and lazy:- If you were not taught while growing up how to be a healthy, well balanced human being, then commitment to self worth and improvement is important. Someone once said, "learn as if you are going to live forever, live as if you are going to die tomorrow."

2. Avoid conflict like the plague:- A disagreement, a difference of opinion, a confrontation, does not mean the end of the relationship. Done with dignity and respect, it can lead to improved communication.

3. Encourage or coerce your partner to tell all then use it against the person.

4. Compromise or reject your values and morals in order to stay in a relationship.

5. See yourself as a victim in every situation: If you feel you have no control then you are powerless to effect change.

❧

6. Deny your personal and family issues while you blame your problems on everything and everyone else. Be irresponsible. It is important that each person accepts responsibility for his or her contribution to a problem and work out a mutual resolution. Always saying "do what makes you happy," does not address or solve the problem.

❧

7. Nurse a basic distrust of your partner: trusting each other is paramount to a healthy well-balanced relationship. Allow each other the opportunity to prove his or her trustworthiness. One's ability to trust is intricately related to the other's proven trustworthiness

❧

8. Believe you can only feel good about yourself and feel happy when you're in an intimate relationship.

ఴ

9. Never develop the ability to move on from the pulse pounding, thrill seeking, head over heels, dizzy phase, to a more mature, caring, comfortable, unconditional love; a safe, secure place to fall, if you will.

ఴ

10. Blame others for your faults and mistakes.

ఴ

11. Never call when you say you will. It's very important to keep your promise. It shows reliability, which is an attractive trait.

ఴ

12. Never show up when you say you will.

ఴ

13. Not recognizing and further discussing '**red flag**' issues but rather assuming love and/or marriage will work out everything.

ભ

14. Be passive aggressive. We should aim to have our verbal and non-verbal responses consistent with the situation.

ભ

15. Don't share feelings and thoughts. **Communication! Communication! Communication!** It's the hallmark of any long lasting relationship,

ભ

16. Walk around on eggshells. I'm speaking metaphorically of course, but you could do it literally to get the true experience. My point is, strive for a level of comfort where you are not afraid to ruffle some feathers, share concerns or even share silly ideas.

ભ

17. Become defensive or aggressive when your comfort zone is touched.

ᢙᢩ

18. Make a pledge to yourself to harbour past hurt anger and resentment.

ᢙᢩ

19. Never allow yourself to grieve the loss and feel the hurt of a failed relationship before getting into another one.

ᢙᢩ

20. Use the word "love/marriage" frivolously to get sex.

ᢙᢩ

21. Use sex to get love. This could imply sex is all you have to offer, which would also imply you are rather uninteresting and quite selfish.

ᢙᢩ

22. Be an unfair person

ᢙᢩ

23. Be selfish and inconsiderate

ፙ

24. Never ask questions or seek clarification

ፙ

25. Be dishonest. Just **Lie, Lie, Lie.**

ፙ

26. Change the rules or make decisions
     without first discussing the issue or possible
     consequences.

ፙ

27. Deny every ounce of emotion you feel, even
     better never be aware of those feelings. If you
     deny your feelings long enough you could
     end up with the tragedy of a dead conscience.
     Nothing bothers you even when it clearly
     should.

ፙ

28. When something is obviously wrong keep saying I'm fine, I'm alright, I'll deal with my problems by myself. Continuously shutting your partners out can lead to isolation and resentment. Its important to respect each others space and response to situations or problems. Coercing someone to talk can push them further away. However, at the same point, some level of connection should be made.

છ૭

29. Rarely discuss or plan activities together. Discussion and planning bring a sense of security to the relationship which is essential for growth.

છ૭

30. Saying you are in a committed relationship though your partner has absolutely no idea where you are or how to contact you for any extended length of time.

છ૭

31.　Spend no time on the relationship. Put no energy into it. By doing this one is unrealistically expecting the relationship to grow into a healthy, loving, lasting one, simply by wishful thinking.

ↄ

32.　Always use sex to pacify issues while never talking about the problem(s).

ↄ

33.　Be a self-centred, controlling and manipulative person who is also an enabler. When there is a strong desire to take over the responsibilities of the other person or you think only of yourself there are bound to be problems.

ↄ

34.　Never ever try to see your partner's point of view or show some empathy. Feeling supported and understood by your partner is like a sprinkler on a garden of flowers.

ↄ

35. Spend little or no time getting to know each other. While there are no guarantees either way, the odds are in your favour and the possibility of surprise is less the more you know about each other.

❧

36. Focus only on immediate gratification instead of long-term satisfaction. Real power is in the ability to control your impulses, not for them to rule you.

❧

37. Break promises just because you can.

❧

38. Be an explorer throughout life, believing the next person is always the right one. I happen to believe each person has his or her own set of problems. You basically swap one set for a different set of problems. The important thing is your tolerance and with what you choose to live.

❧

39.   Have no belief in God or a higher power.

೧

40.   Make physical appearance and or material
      possessions your main criteria on which to
      base a relationship.

೧

41.   Be an unforgiving person. -: Forgiveness is not
      a magic feeling which enters your heart; it's a
      voluntary choice to give up your right to get
      even with the other person or persons.

೧

42.   View problems and difficulties as an easy way
      out, or reason to move on, instead of avenues
      for growth, improved understanding and
      communication.

೧

43.   Embrace the idea that commitment is
      conditional love to a perfect person instead of
      vice versa.

೧

44.   Always expect perfection.

❧

45.   Believe sexual compatibility means today,
       tonight or never. Like parenting, it's a learning
       process.

❧

46.   Believe you can, and will change your partner
       before or after marriage, whether or not the
       person wants to change.

❧

47.   Ignore big, flashing red light, warning signals.
       Take the time to address any situation that
       bothers you.

❧

48.   Hold fast to your own perception of the facts
       regardless of behaviour contrary to the same.
       -: It's important to remember that while we
       are entitled to our own opinions we are not
       entitled to our own facts.

❧

49. Quickly head to a divorce lawyer instead of doing everything you can to work things out such as professional counselling.

☙

50. Don't speak up about things that bother you.

☙

51. Seek only your own satisfaction and gratification in everything.

☙

52. Never ask yourself: "How can I show my love?' 'What can I do?' 'What can I give?" Instead, focus on 'What can I get?' 'What can you do for me'

☙

53. Believe you are always right and don't forget to act that way.

☙

54. Always believe it's my way or the highway. Don't allow for compromise.

☙

55. Make no effort to understand that men and women communicate, receive and reciprocate love differently. -: We all have our love languages, take a moment to find out your partner's and what word or action spells love for him or her.

&

56. Forget the alphabet and never use "I" statements while "you" statements are overused. On the other hand, don't slither into self-centeredness.

&

57. Make no attempt to learn the skills of conflict resolution

&

58. During difficult times, remain emotionally and/or physically distant.

&

59. Refuse to discuss any issue of concern and when your partner tries, make sure you become upset, angry, and defensive.

&

60. Engage in unfair practices in finances and household chores.

❧

61. Hold fast to self-pity and be emotionally needy. -: One way to do this is to bring every situation back to your problem(s).

❧

62. Have emotional and/or physical affair(s)

❧

63. Ignore each other's need for clarification, understanding and security. -: If and when questions are asked, or clarifications are sought, it's helpful to view this as a way to share and improve communication instead of thinking your partner is tricking you into a lie.

❧

64. Be liberal with criticism of your partner, especially when it's audible to others.

❧

65. Be incapable of honesty and make promises you know you will not keep.

❦

66. Whenever a situation becomes uncomfortable, scary or difficult, run away, without realizing that this thinking and attitude will keep you running for the rest of your life.

❦

67. Mythically make yourself the center of your universe. -: If I don't think it or feel it, you shouldn't either.

❦

68. Focus only on your sexual satisfaction. -: Selfishness has no place here. It's like a pile of bricks that keeps getting higher and thicker. It builds resentment and anger.

❦

69. Never grow up!

❦

70. Allow your parents to treat you like a child, manipulate and control you. -: It's important to stand up for yourself and not be afraid to disagree with, or confront your parent(s) if and when the situation requires it; and especially if one or both disrespect your partner. Without successful resolution of certain parental issues one might be incapable of finding a marriage partner.

ᗐ

71. Put each other last on your list of priorities. -: Knowing you matter to someone is a very comforting feeling.

ᗐ

72. Be kind, helpful and generous to practically everyone except your partner.

ᗐ

73. **Interrogate, Interrogate, Interrogate!** -: This can stem from the fear of being hurt or the need to protect one's heart from breaking: but it quickly can become destructive.

ᗐ

74. Work hard at helping others not to rely on you.

೮ఌ

75. Be jealousy that goes beyond the normal healthy appreciation of caring for, and protecting what is yours.

೮ఌ

76. Lack of self- esteem. -: Lack of a strong healthy self-concept often motivates us to either overcompensate or under-compensate; which fosters a belief that we are not important. I believe self-concept, which begins in infancy and develops through our early years, is an important factor in forming our personality structure and the mental map, if you will, which guides our behaviour. Our success in life is related to it.

೮ఌ

77. Maintain a strong desire to take over the responsibility of another person. -: This unhealthy enmeshment encourages bad, negative and/or potentially harmful behaviour to continue by making it easier for the person engaging in such behaviour, as well as meets one of many needs in the other such as control.

℘

78. Insist on viewing your partner through your eyes only, believing your thoughts and feeling should be his or hers. -: This should also lead to a situation where, though you choose not to do or ask for something, your partner is accused of self-centred behaviour if and when he or she does.

℘

79. Don't tell your partner what you want, what you need, what makes you feel loved, special, or valued; just pray desperately he or she becomes psychic Sue/Sam or just read your mind. Become angry and disappointed when that doesn't happen. On the other hand, I believe it is important for us to strive to improve on our emotional intelligence, which enables us to read other people's emotions without getting verbal specifics. It's truly a beneficial life skill.

೧

80. Don't make the effort to find out what each other likes. Don't make the effort to do it.

೧

81. Don't be nice, polite, or kind to each other; which is the way we usually are with strangers and acquaintances. -: It is understandable that we tend to choose a safe place to vent our frustration, disappointment and anger about everyday stressors. That safe place is often the people we love and who are closest to us. Overdoing this can be damaging so let's try to treat our loved ones with the pleasant courtesy we extend to strangers.

೧

82.   Do not establish healthy boundaries. -:
      Owning our behaviours, feelings and attitudes
      is essential to any relationship. It's important
      to know when to say, "It's not business as
      usual".

                    ∾

83.   Constantly nag and/or argue with each other.
      -: if most of our conversations end in bitter
      arguments then be aware joy is dying a slow
      painful death.

                    ∾

84.   Violate each other's trust.

                    ∾

85. Become and stay addicted to anything, even yourself. -: Continued addiction to anything leads to ruined lives and families. There's always an emotional root to an addiction. Find out yours and deal with it. It's often the created result of our decisions and contributes to suspension of rationality and good judgment. One example is pornography, which, contrary to popular belief is not a victimless crime. In fact this is a fatal attraction, which gives permission to treat women and children in a degrading manner. Men are dominant and seek only their own gratification. You are actually sharing your relationship with several other people and there's no way to compete. When this mind set is taken into a relationship, It's no surprise your partner will feel used. Any addiction (porn, gambling, drugs, etc.) will cause devastating pain and hurt.

86. Be disrespectful to each other.

87. Continue to tolerate behaviours that violate the relationship. -: it's important to not view your relationship in all or nothing manner. That is, I'll accept intolerable behaviour and do nothing or get a divorce; instead, begin to invoke consequences for behaviour and maintain boundaries.

88. Correct each other in public. -: Support each other all the way and be each other's refuge. In private you can be each other's worst enemy, within reasons of course.

89. Have no confidence in each other.

90. Stay stuck in the phase of "freedom" of uncommitment. -: If one is to negotiate through life successfully towards greater maturity, certain desires, conditions and attitudes must be given up.

91. Keep score and don't make it a habit to forgive each other. -: To borrow the words of another, "relationships thrive not because the guilty are punished but because the innocent are merciful."

92. Desert each other when you face trouble, difficulties, problems or hardships. -: It's very important to be each other's refuge and support. Stand by each other and show love to each other; it's, after all, an action word. Love is as love does, it's effortful, not effortless. To be loving we must go beyond desire, extend ourselves, have the will and choose to do so.

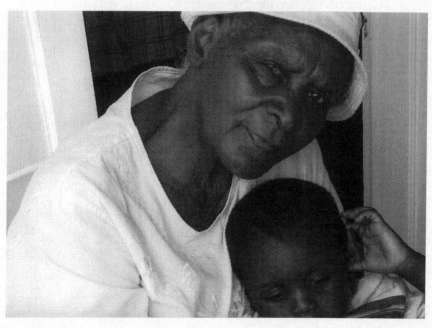

Your friends are going to disappoint you. You have to forgive them for this.
(Adapted)

A guilty conscience needs no accuser.
(Charmaine Richards)

Love is a decision of the will carried out by actions with warm feelings not merely a fleeting feeling.
(Charmaine Richards)

> *We are not always right but it's not because we are always wrong.*
> *(Adapted)*

> *We can easily forgive a child who's afraid of the dark; the real tragedy of life is when men are afraid of the light.*
> *(Adapted)*

Sometimes the persons we claim to know
the best are the ones that surprise us the most.
(Adapted)

In a time of universal deceit, telling
the truth is a revolutionary act.
(Adapted)

> *Delay is the deadliest form of denial.*
> *(Adapted)*

> *We can't change the direction of the wind, but we can adjust our sail to always reach our destination.*
> *(Adapted)*

The first effect of not believing in God
is that you lose your common sense.
(Adapted)

If a man doesn't believe in God, he doesn't
believe in nothing and he believes in anything.
(Adapted)

Be kind. Everyone is fighting a great battle.
(Adapted)

The deeper the pain, the higher the debt.
(Oprah Winfrey)

Intelligence plus character,
that is the goal of true education.
(Charmaine Richards)

Good prosecutors get convictions,
great ones get justice.
(Adapted)

*The life of the dead lives on
in the memory of the living.
(Adapted)*

*Out of suffering emerge the strongest souls. The
most amazing characters are seared with scars.
(Adapted)*

If there must be trouble let it be in my time so my children can be at peace. (Adapted)

> *Of all the animals, man is the only one that is cruel. Man is the only one who inflicts pain for the pleasure of doing it.*
> *(Adapted)*

> *Having people love you and loving them back is the greatest gift of all, and can even overcome biology.*
> *(Charmaine Richards)*

The seed we plant predicts the
type of crop we harvest.
(Adapted)

> *Many people have the wrong concept of true happiness. It's not attained through self-gratification. True happiness is fidelity to a worthy purpose. (Adapted)*

> *Luck is often preparation meeting opportunity. (Adapted)*

He ain't heavy... he's my brother.

*What the caterpillar calls the end of the world...the master calls a butterfly.
(Adapted)*

*Be not afraid of growing slowly;
be afraid only of standing still.
(Adapted)*

*To love oneself is the beginning
of a lifelong romance.
(Adapted)*

*All beginnings require that
you unlock a new door.
(Adapted)*

> *A true friend is someone who
> can make us do what we can.
> (Adapted)*

> *Not everything that is faced can be changed
> but...nothing can be changed, unless it is faced.
> (Adapted)*

There are only two options regarding commitment you're either IN or you're OUT. There's no such thing as life in-between. (Adapted)

Having nothing is far better than being in debt.
(Charmaine Richards)

Men heap together the mistakes of their lives
and create a monster they call destiny.
(Adapted)

*If you can't bear the thought of messing up
your tidy little soul, then you won't make
it as a human being.
(Adapted)*

*Nothing is easier than denouncing the evil doer,
nothing more difficult than understanding him.
(Adapted)*

The best kind of friends is the kind you can sit on a porch and swing with, never say a word, then walk away feeling like it was the best conversation you've ever had. (Adapted)

Good health cultivates happiness.
(Adapted)

Good friends are like stars. You don't always see them but you know they are always there. (Adapted)

Good friends are like a well orchestrated symphony, regardless of time and distance, once contact is made, it's like no beat missed, no time lapsed. (Adapted)

Giving someone all your love is never an assurance that they'll love you back! Don't expect love in return; just wait for it to grow in their heart, but if it doesn't, be content it grew in yours. (Adapted)

It can take only a minute to get a crush on someone, an hour to like someone, and a day to love someone; but it can take a lifetime to forget someone. (Adapted)

It's true that sometimes we don't know what we've got until it's gone; but it's also true that sometimes we don't know what we've been missing until it arrives. (Adapted)

Heartbreak is truly both emotional and physical pain. (Charmaine Richards)

*Good parenting is one of the most difficult
and challenging, yet the most fulfilling,
rewarding and joyful job I know.
(Adapted)*

Children are simply angels until age 10…
after that they are …"see next book"
(Charmaine Richards)

Watch a sunrise...... watch a sunset.
(Charmaine Richards)

Safety is the presence of God
not the absence of danger.
(Adapted)

*There is no witness so damaging no
accuser so dreadful as the conscience
that lives inside a man.*
(Adapted)

Mercy bears richer fruits than strict justice.
(Abraham Lincoln)

Be not afraid of what you may or do not know, be more afraid of what you know for sure that isn't so. (Adapted)

Before you embark on a journey of revenge, dig two graves.
(Adapted)

Needless to say, if you avoid or work to resolve the aforementioned problems and scenarios, you'll be on your way to a happy, long-lasting, loving and fulfilling relationship. Have fun getting there and even more pleasure as you can continue your "work in progress". The ability of two persons to share their lives with each other, with all their "baggage", vices, and idiosyncrasies, is to me, one of God's most precious gifts. He wants us to have loving, joyful relationships. He actually started the first one in the lovely garden. Unfortunately the high divorce rate seems to tell a different story.

Let's get away from the "me, myself and I" mentality where we think: "I'm not happy, things aren't going my way, things are little inconvenient for me, let me end things or get a divorce so I can find someone else to make me happy." Let's instead embrace the concept of commitment and the permanence of marriage.

God intended our relationship to be a life long one, regardless of sickness, trials, financial reversal, hardship or emotional stresses that may ensue. It is truly the more excellent way!

He Still Cares

Though your plans are broken your pain cannot be spoken
Again you're lost and defeated somehow you feel you've been cheated.
Just remember Jesus cares, all your burdens
He promised to bear, He's not like man, He understands.
He still cares.

Although your faith is shaken, your steps feel like they're taken
Your emotions run wild 'cause your life you can't reconcile
He has the future in His hand, the universe is at His command
He's always near, do not despair
He still cares.

Though you'd like to surrender, you're tired of battles and strife
There's no joy in your heart, you wonder why it's still dark
Jesus loves you and He cares, He knows how much you can bear
He's your light and your way, your hope and your stay
He still cares.

Know that He loves you and He cares
All your problems He's promised to share
He's not like man, He understands,
He still cares
He's got the future in His hand, the universe is at His command
He is your way, your hope and your stay
He still cares

Just try my Jesus 'cause He cares, He knows how much you can bear
He is right here, do not despair
He still cares
As for Peter, He has prayed that your faith will not fail
You're in His hand, His prayer stands
He still cares.

written by Angela Smith

Recipe for Rock Cakes

Ingredients

12 ounces flour

6 ounces sugar

6 ounces fat (margarine or butter)

1 level tablespoon baking powder

½ teaspoon grated nutmeg

½ cup grated /shredded coconut

2 eggs

¼ cup raisin (optional)

Method

1. Sieve flour with baking powder

2. Rub margarine into flour until it resembles cornmeal or fine bread crumbs

3. Add other ingredients except egg

4. Beat eggs lightly then add some to mixture gradually

5. Combine to make a thick dough. If necessary add remainder of egg gradually. N.B. Mixture should be a stiff dough

6. Drop in rocky heap on greased baking tray

7. **Bake at 350 °F until done**. (Approximately 15-20mins)

Submitted by: Beverley Peart